Legendary
IRELAND

Legendary
IRELAND

TOM KELLY
Photographs

PETER SOMERVILLE-LARGE
Text

TOWN HOUSE PUBLISHERS
Dublin, Ireland

ROBERTS RINEHART PUBLISHERS
Boulder, Colorado

Published in the US and Canada by Roberts Rinehart Publishers,
5455 Spine Road, Boulder, Colorado 80301

Distributed by Publishers Group West

ISBN 1–57098–048–9

Published in Ireland by Town House and Country House Publishers,
Trinity House, Charleston Road, Ranelagh, Dublin 6, Ireland

ISBN 0–946172–52–8

Library of Congress Catalog Card No. 95–69272

A CIP record for this book is available from the British Library

Front cover photograph: Bective Abbey, County Meath

Back cover photograph: Clonmacnoise, County Offaly

Sources: *Pre-Christian Ireland–From the First Settlers to the Early Celts*, Peter Harbison,
Thames and Hudson, 1994; *Over Nine Waves*, Marie Heaney, Faber and Faber, 1994;
Twenty Years in the Wild West or Life in Connaught, Mrs. M.C. Houston, London, 1879;
The New Oxford Book of Irish Verse, Thomas Kinsella (ed), Oxford University Press, 1986.

Design: Frederick R. Rinehart and Jack Van Zandt

Editors: Elaine Campion and Mary Hegarty

Typesetting: Red Barn Publishing, Skeagh, Skibbereen, Co. Cork, Ireland

Set in Galliard 12/16 pt

Printed in Hong Kong by COLORCORP/Sing Cheong

CONTENTS

Graves of the Leinstermen, County Tipperary

The Dawn of Time

Doo Lough, County Mayo

*T*he symbiosis of pagan and Christian tradition in Ireland was a long and painfully worked out compromise imposed by nature. On a wild island at the edge of Europe the mysteries of wind, weather and landscape had evolved for thousands of years in animistic beliefs in the power of many gods and goddesses. These pagan beliefs had to be blended into an alien religion brought from the shores of the Mediterranean. Not only the influences of isolated surroundings, but deeper pulses of paganism are imbued in the Irish character beyond the reaches of religious orthodoxy.

The storms that come rolling from the Atlantic, the long winter days and nights, clear summer mornings and autumn mists, all combine to form a foundation for beliefs that ultimately depended on the pathetic fallacy—that nature's moods reflect our own joys and sorrows.

Christianity took a long time to incorporate ancient beliefs and customs and denigrate them to "folklore", but it could not wholly suppress them. Old tales and the spoken word have been handed down through generations; the *seanchaí* or storyteller sitting in front of a glowing turf fire did his work in time to preserve a collective memory that some people say stretches back to Noah.

From Noah's time the restless forces of nature in a country where wind and weather, light and shade change from day to day or hour to hour, demanded an explanation in religion and myth. If today's weather forecasters, even with the most modern scientific measurements and satellites, can be mistaken in their calculations, it is not surprising that our ancestors relied on ancient beliefs to explain the nature of Irish climate. Predictions about the weather were part of Celtic belief.

Thunder and lightning, a sudden fall of snow, were more than physical phenomena; they expressed the attributes of the gods. The shrieks of Aoife, punished for enchanting the children of Lir, can be heard in a gale. Christianity had to confront the powers of Boan the water goddess, Manannán Mac Lir the god of the seas, and Lugh the sun god.

*L*ike the weather, the landscape of Ireland was infinitely changeable and formidable, as rivers, mountains, forests and bog competed for the terrain. In legend, rivers were diverted by magic powers. There are frequent moments in Celtic legend when heroes have to confront the bog and forest. The bog, for all the beauty placed upon it by bog cotton flowering in early summer, was a threatening waste; the forest was an impassable barrier, a home to enemies and wolves. King Aillil bargained that the price of his daughter's hand would be the draining of twelve great bogs and the levelling of twelve forests. At Tara, King Eochaí similarly demanded that when young Midir lost a game on his silver jewel-studded board, his forfeit should be the cutting down of seven forests, reclaiming seven hundred acres of bog and making seven causeways through them.

Midlands thunderstorm

Tír na nÓg, land of eternal youth

A clearing storm at sunset

West Cork rainbow

*E*verywhere, great and lesser figures of legend touch the landscape. Spirits include Daghdha, leader of the Tuatha de Danaan, Boan the water goddess, and Manannán Mac Lir the god of the seas, who wore a magical water suit made from leaves. Lugh the sun god wore the Milky Way as a silver chain round his neck, and carried a sword called the Answerer and a rainbow as his sling.

The beauty of nature's rainbow has given it a sacred significance in ancient legends. In the Orient, the rainbow is an important attribute of the benevolent goddess Tara, as it is worked into her halo. In Roman mythology, Iris, the attendant of Juno, queen of the gods, was the personification of the rainbow; one of her functions was to release the souls of women struggling in the pangs of death. Her beauty was enhanced by her filmy clothes shining in a weave of violet, indigo, blue, green, yellow, orange and red. Perhaps the elusive nature of the rainbow as a feature of this island's changeable weather has precluded it from taking a more prominent part in Irish mythology. The well-known legend of the pot of gold emphasizes the shifting nature of the spectrum's most dramatic effects. Lugh's sling is a rapid and fearsome weapon, which appears in victory as the sun wins the struggle to overcome the rain.

Reflections

Glencar, County Sligo

Fog over bogland, County Donegal

Gods and goddesses and their subsequent Christian personifications dominated the year's cycle, which depended on the length of days and the division of the year into six-month periods, marked by the feasts of Bealtaine and Samhain. In due course the four major festivals associated with the seasons were grafted onto Christianity.

Imbolg, the first day of February, was associated with the deity that controlled the rhythms of growth and harvest, the earthmother goddess whose Celtic forms were Macha, Danu and Bríde. As the goddess Bríde, she was brought into the Christian fold, assuming the virgin role that was appropriate to a religion dominated by chastity. The blend of Christianity and pagan belief is neatly incorporated at Downpatrick, County Down, where Brigid is said to be buried beside Ireland's two great missionary saints.

Three saints one grave do fill:
Patrick, Brigid and Columcille.

Innumerable girls are still given the name of a saint whose attributes are imbued with traditional magic. Her day marks the beginning of spring. "On St. Brigid's Day," the saying ran, "You can put away the candlestick and half the candle." Her Celtic origins are recalled in the making of the

Crios Bríde or girdle, the *Brídeog* or fertility doll, and her association with flowers and birds that include the oyster catcher and the lark. A lark singing on St. Brigid's Day was an omen of a good spring. As the goddess connected with fertility, she had a regard for all livestock, and her festival coincides with changes in the farming year when ewes come into milk.

The festival of Bealtaine, held on May Eve and the first day of May, marked the start of summer, an important time on the farm, when cattle were driven between bonfires as part of a purification rite. The weather on May Day was significant: "a wet and windy May fills the barns with corn and hay." May dew, good for sore eyes and headaches, was an aid to beauty.

I washed my face in water
That had neither rained nor run
And I dried it on a towel
That was never woven nor spun.

Folklore and pagan belief similarly surrounded the midsummer festivals and Lúnasa, the time of outdoor gatherings which marks harvest's beginning. Samhain, on the last day of October, which survives as Hallowe'en, was a day for feasting and merrymaking, to celebrate the safe gathering in of the crops.

No farmer or fisherman could ignore the weather signs that came with these festivals nor the customs associated with survival. Although there have been hard changes in country life during the past fifty years as modern technology and the bulldozer do their destructive work, country-folk still retain their ancestors' reverence for the land that they work and the seasonal changes which affect their life and livelihood.

Winter in County Mayo

Spring, Ladies View, Ring of Kerry

Rich midland pasture in summer

Monaincha, County Tipperary

Markers on the Landscape

Natural Markers

Mountains, lakes, rivers, bogs and forests, different aspects of the spectacular and desolate patchwork that was the island of Ireland, all played their part in pre-Christian myth and belief. Today's traveler can best capture a feeling for these ancient mysteries by seeking out the varied mountain ranges and spectacular cliffs that ring the island. Stand on the Cliffs of Moher in Co. Clare or Benwee Head on the northwest coast of Co. Mayo on a stormy day when the spray from the crashing waves blots out the sky. The saddle line of the Twelve Pins in Connemara, Co. Galway, rising above the bog, the surviving oak forests around Killarney, Co. Kerry, and the limestone escarpments of the Burren in Co. Clare are homes for the gods and settings for ancient legends.

Certain distinctive mountains were a focus of legend. In north Kerry, two startlingly symmetrical peaks were naturally interpreted as the breasts of the earth goddess Danu. One of the most enchanted hills in Ireland is Slievenamon, whose solitary high dome hangs over Co. Tipperary. Maidens raced up this "Hill of Women" to the summit to win the hand of Finn MacCool. Traditionally the home of the fairies, Slievenamon was where heroes like Finn MacCool, Oisín and Oscar assembled. The fairy mountain has obstinately resisted Christian baptism and remains a pagan place. As late as 1890 occurred the sombre killing of a woman believed to have been possessed by the little people who lived on its slopes.

By contrast, Croagh Patrick in Co. Mayo, a holy mountain long before the arrival of Ireland's patron on these shores, succumbed easily to the new faith. Its long association with St. Patrick has resulted in a spectacular Christian ritual, the ascent on Garland Sunday, the last Sunday in July.

Cliffs of Moher, County Clare

Benwee, County Mayo

Tully Mountains, County Galway

Twelve Pins, Connemara

Dingle, County Kerry

Burren, County Clare

Connemara

Croagh Patrick, County Mayo

Conor Pass, County Kerry

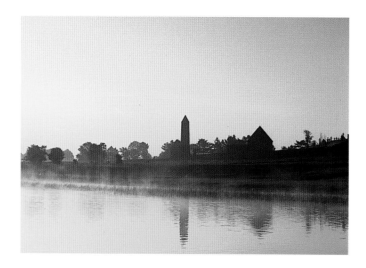

River Shannon at Clonmacnoise

The rivers of Ireland, the Boyne, Liffey, Nore, Slaney, Shannon and many others, were personified as gods and goddesses, perhaps most familiar to us as the stylized faces on Gandon's keystones around Dublin's Custom House. Enchanted spirits lurked under lakes. At Lough Gur in Co. Limerick the Earl of Desmond rides over the water every seven years on his silver-shod horse. Here legend is bolstered by archeological evidence of great age. The horseshoe lake with its waterbirds and swans lies in the midst of limestone hills, with the knuckles of Knockadoon and Knockfennel rising to east and west. It is the central focus of an area crammed with traces of Stone Age or Early Christian peoples. Wherever you look they unfold before your eyes. Here is a ring fort, there a partially destroyed megalithic tomb, *Leaba na Muice*, the Pig's Bed. A *crannóg* (artificial island dwelling) surrounded by rushes floats on the lake, and the house sites along its shore include the elaborate Spectacles, a formation so called because of its shape, reminiscent of reading glasses. A Neolithic cemetery and the largest *lios* or stone

ring in the country offer further evidence that the strategic combination of lake and hill, its rich limestone pasture cleared of forest, had special attraction for prehistoric society.

A fertile area like Lough Gur naturally drew a rural population away from the wastes of bog. In geological terms the spread of bog is a rapid phenomenon, and over the past few thousand years it covered tracts of fertile land. Much of Ireland was overlaid with expanding raised bog, a never-ending source of fuel, and the all-encompassing blanket-bog. From time to time blanket-bog recedes to reveal secrets of the past, ranging from ancient tree pollens to artifacts of Neolithic man. Retreating bog on Mount Gabriel in Co. Cork has uncovered quarries where stone mauls and charcoal are revealed as detritus from copper mines that can be dated back to 1500 B.C. Calcified bog butter, the occasional preserved body, dried stumps of ancient forest, or antlers of the extinct Irish elk, have been found in bog. One of the most splendid of recent finds has been the Derrynaflan Chalice, raised from a bog in Co. Tipperary.

New discoveries which interpret how Neolithic farmers cultivated their lands have been less spectacular but more informative about our distant past. The Céide Fields in Co. Mayo and the field patterns uncovered on Clare Island off the Mayo coast, until recently swallowed up by blanket-bog, have revealed elaborate details of Neolithic settlements, court cairns, and field systems, marked by grooved lines of fields and stone walls. Traces of houses and scratched marks made by primitive ploughs and digging sticks provide links with the land that has been cultivated for six thousand years.

Lough Gill, County Sligo

Lough Gur, County Limerick

Lake on Mizen Head, West Cork

Killary Harbour, County Mayo

West Cork trees

From the time that humans arrived in Ireland thousands of years ago, forest was the farmer's enemy. After the glaciers receded, willows and birches formed the first woodlands, to be followed by hazel. As the first settlers became established, scrub forest, with copses of intervening oak, elm and birch, had to be cleared for pasture for cattle. Areas surrounding Neolithic settlements had to be marked out for the planting of rough weed-infested cereal crops.

It was natural that some trees of the surrounding unfriendly forest should take on magical properties. Yew, a greenish-black native conifer, living to a great age, with hard timber and red berries, was a sacred tree. Its timber was used for croziers and book shrines. Rowan likewise was regarded as a protector. Ivy, with its autumn flowers and mournful color, was another plant with magic powers.

"Holly and hazel, elder and rowan and bright ash from beside the ford..." Trees like St. Kevin's yew tree at Glendalough, Co. Wicklow, and St. Brigid's oak at Kildare, which she loved and blessed, had a significance for saints. Holy trees have refused to die and miraculously renew themselves. St. Fintan's money tree in Co. Laois still shows its branch coated with coins. Near to where I live in Co. Kilkenny, St. Molling's well is attended by an ash tree of great age and sanctity, a cutting, perhaps, of a tree that predated the saint himself.

Warrenstown, County Meath

Connemara

Clare/Galway border

*T*he people of Ireland, struggling to survive in a landscape that was a blend of majesty and desolation, evolved a unique set of beliefs that blended with their surroundings. Recognition of the power of fire, the healing qualities of water and rivers, respect for fairy hills and holy mountains, the purification induced by pilgrimage, reverence for sacred trees, certain rocks and stones, and holy wells whose waters were deemed to have healing powers, were all manifestations of ancient and continuing identity with the world of nature.

Over the centuries poverty, doctrinal differences, famine and eviction did not weaken acceptance of ancient doctrines. On the contrary, it has been suggested that the persistence of pagan beliefs, particularly in remote places, was a reaction against the drab reality of people's lives. Poverty and hardship could be transformed over the generations with the myth and magic of fairyland. Customs that had vanished from other European countries were preserved in Ireland in a rich store of memories.

Glenmalure, County Wicklow

Human-made Markers

A great pleasure for my friend Dan O'Brien who lived on the Beara peninsula in Co. Cork was the chasing of dolmens. On any fine summer's morning he would hear the news, "I've heard from a farmer there's an interesting alignment only a few miles from here." He would jump into his car and vanish up a boreen thick in fuchsia, and make his way around Beara's bony hills, which in summer are covered in furze and thorn. Hours later he would return to his cottage near Eyeries with news of his latest discovery. A map was taken out and the new site proclaimed. It might be a ring fort hidden in bracken, a standing stone or the outline of a broken ring of stones. Beara is only one remote place in Ireland where stone traces of past civilization still wait to be brought to light. Year by year the past continues to yield its secrets; one of the most recent—the observation of Neolithic field patterns in Co. Mayo—is a discovery only of the last decade.

The earliest known traces of humans in Ireland, dating to around 7000 B.C., are found in areas like Mount Sandel, Co. Derry, and along the Bann river in Co. Down. These Mesolithic farmers and gatherers built simple structures of wood and sod, which even contained a small hearth; they used flint as a tool and a weapon and left very little behind them.

Neolithic peoples arrived some thousands of years later, along with their farming methods. Around the newcomers' settlements the forests were ring-barked and cut down to make way for livestock and arable cultivation. From that time until the Christian era, legendary Ireland and its mysteries evolved.

*"L*et the stones speak," says the archeologist. In a country where so much suffers the attrition of weather and war, it is the stones that survive, waiting to be unearthed. Ruins are part of our psyche. Castles, plundered abbeys and tiny churches are part of the stone litter. Traces of cottages and cabins provide poignant evidence of abandoned struggles with poverty. Sometimes the remains of whole villages survive.

One village lies eerily intact on the south flanks of Slievemore Mountain on Achill Island in Co. Mayo. A line of roofless cabins stretches beside a mile-long street—there are said to be a hundred of them. It appears as if a whole community suddenly deserted their homes, leaving these empty shells. The Irish trilogy of famine, emigration and eviction has been suggested for this ghostly maze of stone walling, and perhaps a combination of all three was the explanation. Abandoned some time in the late nineteenth century, for decades they continued to be a location for booley houses, temporary living quarters during summer months when cattle were seeking summer pastures.

Deserted village, Achill Island, County Mayo

Fallen stones, Mount Leinster

The *gallán*, or standing stone, is the most common surviving field monument. These monoliths vary from the nineteen-foot giant at Punchestown, Co. Kildare, to stones with holes cut in them or fringed with the patterned strokes of Ogham writing. Some are prominently placed, like the Graves of the Leinstermen above Lough Derg in Co. Tipperary. Others are spectacular because of their numbers. A few miles from Roscrea, Co. Tipperary, is the location of the most concentrated groups of standing stones in Ireland.

You find them suddenly near the crossroads at Inch.

"There's not much to see anyway," said the farmer starting up his tractor when I visited the site in winter. But there is, and they are little known. Tramping through muddy fields I discovered dozens, up to three or four hundred stones assembled without apparent pattern, some standing, others lying on the grass, covered with lichen and moss. Who knows now as they lie under tattered gray skies their ancient cultural significance?

Mermaid stone, Crukancornia, County Sligo

Piper's Stones, County Wicklow

Stone circles are another source of mystery about which we have to make guesses. The legend of the Piper's Stones postdates by many centuries the setting up of this ring at Athgreany in Co. Wicklow. The piper and those who danced to his tune were turned to stone for profaning the Sabbath. The alignment of many circles seems to relate to the solstice, and a few like Drombeg in Co. Cork have been measured and estimated to be pointing towards the place where the winter sun first rises after the December darkness. But the proof is by no means precise.

Drombeg stone circle, County Cork

Stone circle, County Cork

Lisvigeen stone circle, County Kerry

Following page: Poulnabrone, County Clare

Lough Crew, County Meath

Browne's Hill, County Carlow

There is clearer evidence that dolmens and court cairns were erected as the result of an elaborate burial culture. Armies of people and great earthworks must have been needed to get these giant structures into position. Some, for example the dolmen at Harristown, Co. Kilkenny, are like giant card houses which threaten to collapse after thousands of years.

The dolmen at Browne's Hill in Co. Carlow, an impressive giant facing the encroachment of suburbia, still manages to look magnificent, with its vast capstone weighing over a hundred tons. Poulnabrone, standing starkly on Burren limestone in Co. Clare, has a surreal air, as if the twentieth-century painter Dali placed it there. Within this tomb archeologists have found not only the usual artifacts like flints and scrapers, but the communal bones of twenty-two adults and six children.

At Loughcrew in Co. Meath, thirty or forty tombs are sited on a treeless mountain. On the last day I was there a roaring wind played

around Slieve na Callaigh, or the Hill of the Witch. Westward in Co. Sligo, the Labby is propped up against a farmer's wall, its giant capstone decorated with a cap of gorse and heather. Its bizarre appearance has led it to be called the clown of Irish dolmens. Near the Labby are traces of another great Neolithic cemetery, Carrowkeel, on the limestone ridges of the Bricklieve mountains overlooking Lough Arrow. These tombs have kept their silence and remoteness, unvisited except by grazing sheep and the occasional hawk fluttering its wings. By comparison, the Neolithic tombs of Carrowmore near Sligo have been trivialized by the bungalows and houses creeping around them; these ancient graveyards are places asking for silence.

Labby Rock, County Sligo

Carrowmore, County Sligo

Carrowmore, County Sligo

Three Castle Head, West Cork

Aileach, County Donegal

Aileach, County Donegal

Hill of Uisnach, County Westmeath

The majority of raths which we see today stem from the Christian period. They were simple homesteads, their earthen walls providing protection from wolves and cattle raiders. Although in recent times many have become victims to the bulldozer, it has been estimated that thirty to forty thousand have managed to survive.

While most of these earthen forts served as homesteads, cashels built in stone offered far more elaborate defense. Staigue Fort in Co. Kerry, with its stairways leading to terraces, is a magnificent example of a stone ring fort. On Aran Mór, the largest of the Aran Islands off Co. Galway, the great cashel of Dún Aengus is a half moon of boulders poised at the edge of a cliff. In Co. Donegal the Grianán of Aileach stands among eroded earthworks, the chief fort of the Uí Néill, descendants of Niall of the Nine Hostages. Destroyed by

Murrough O'Brien, king of Munster, in revenge for the destruction of Kincora, enough stones survived for this "Fort of the Sun" to be reconstructed in the late nineteenth century.

Celtic royalties and deities have left their stamp on elaborate earthworks. Crowning the Hill of Ward in Co. Meath, the palace of Tlachta can be traced by four rings of ramparts. The name Tlachta derives from that of a sorceress who died in childbirth and was buried here. In pre-Christian times, annual assemblies at the beginning of winter, a time when spirits are always said to wander on the earth—hence Hallowe'en, involved rituals which are reputed to have included human sacrifice.

In neighboring Co. Westmeath, the Hill of Uisneach has traces of the palace of King Tuathal of Connacht; in addition, here is the location of the Cat-Usnagh, a limestone boulder known in ancient times as *Aill na Mireann*, the Stone of Divisions. Determining the center of the island, the Welsh monk Geraldus Cambrensis called the Cat Stone the Navel of Ireland. At the feast of Bealtaine a great fair was held on the Hill of Uisneach, together with ceremonies incorporating fire and incantations for the safeguard of cattle. Chieftains were required to present their horses and trappings to the king of Connacht.

None of these locations competes with the majesty evoked by the name of Tara, the seat of the high kings until it was abandoned by Máel Sechnaill in 1022. This natural fortress on its lonely hill has views which stretch across the midlands to far off mountain ranges in Leinster, Munster, Connacht and Ulster. Tara not only was the site for the palace of Celtic kings, with subsequent associations with St. Patrick, but was also used by Neolithic peoples as a cemetery. Over eighty identifiable monuments have been located on the site, including Neolithic chambered tombs, Bronze Age burials and Iron Age raths.

The Mound of the Hostages, Gráinne's fort, the fort of the kings and the site of the famous banqueting hall, leave faint traces of vanished glory. Like the Hill of Uisneach, its location accounted for its importance; here was the center of the ancient division of Ireland into five provinces where all roads met. From Tara, the druid or high king, Cormac the Wise, had the comforting feeling that he ruled the whole island.

Tara has history enough to be the focus for lament and loss. But Ireland's greatest stoneworks, the triumvirate passage tombs of Newgrange, Dowth and Knowth, scattered along the river Boyne in Co. Meath, predate history. Although excavation has shown the complicated techniques used in the construction of Newgrange to have involved two hundred thousand tons of stone, these burial places are still mysterious. Theories have been put forward concerning druidical rites, links with ancestral spirits and the suggestion that this is the place where heaven and earth meet. Newgrange was the grave of Aengus, the Celtic god of love, and the river Boyne passing below was worshipped as a goddess.

Here the winter solstice was observed annually, as the newly risen sun trickled through the long passageway. It continues to make the annual journey, and today the privileged are allowed to witness the movement of the solstice on the twenty-first of December as the days begin to

Newgrange, County Meath

lengthen once more. There is an eight-year waiting list for those who wish to enter the chamber on that day, but often the weather is not cooperative and the sun is hidden in cloud.

The best way to see Newgrange is from the river, as Tom Kelly pictures it. Some years ago, a friend and I rowed down from above Slane, and at the slow turn of the Boyne we landed under the brooding dome, which in those days had not been refaced in white quartz, an imaginative reconstruction of the way it looked four thousand five hundred years ago. There was no car park then, but even now, when Newgrange has become a tourist center, the "glittering temple of the dead" is an astonishing place.

Like Slievenamon, Newgrange remained pagan; Patrick did not step this way beside the Boyne. But a few miles away the Hill of Slane overlooks another stretch of the Boyne. Thousands of years after the worshippers of the Boyne valley tumuli watched the vital change of the year, St. Patrick lit the Paschal fire on the summit of this little hill in defiance of King Laoghaire's decree.

Rock of Dunamace, County Laois

75

St. Patrick defies Royal Tara

After spending six years in slavery in Ireland, Patrick escaped to the continent, where he trained as a missionary. He returned to Ireland as a bishop to convert the people to Christianity. He arrived in Leinster on the eve of Bealtaine, or May Day, which was held sacred and was traditionally marked by a pagan rite to the sun. All fires were extinguished on May eve and none could be lit until dawn when the high king ignited a great fire on the Hill of Tara.

Patrick decided to defy the high king's decree. On the nearby hill of Slane, he lit a Paschal fire to celebrate the eve of Easter. His followers helped him pile up the fuel to create a great blaze. King Laoghaire saw the flames rising high into the air. Furious at this challenge to his authority, he demanded, "Who has dared to light this fire?" His druids replied, "We do not know who lit it, but unless it is put out quickly it will never be extinguished. Its light will eclipse our sacred fires and the man who ignited it will have power over us all, even over the high king himself."

King Laoghaire ordered his warriors to bring the man to him. They hurried to Slane and brought Patrick and his monks to the court of the high king. When they arrived at Tara, Laoghaire immediately sentenced Patrick to death.

Patrick showed no fear. He declared, "Christ is the true sun and he will never die. He will give eternal life to those who do his will." He explained that there was only one God but that he was three persons: the Father, the Son, and the Holy Spirit. The druids were skeptical so, to illustrate the mystery of the Trinity, Patrick bent down and plucked a sprig of shamrock. "Here is one stem but there are three leaves. Likewise, there is one God but three persons stemming from the same divinity." King Laoghaire was impressed. He withdrew the death sentence and gave Patrick permission to preach his gospel throughout Ireland. Although many of his court became Christians, Laoghaire did not himself convert to Christianity, preferring to uphold the ancient traditions and culture of the Irish people.

Hill of Tara, County Meath

Christianity was already established in Ireland for several centuries before the arrival of Patrick. It was a creed with a particularly Hibernian slant, fostered by saints and hermits. They derived their spiritual awareness as much from nature as from their books and religious exercises.

The hermit Marban informed King Guaire:

I have a hut here in the wood
that nobody knows but my Lord.
An ash tree one side is its wall,
the other a hazel, a great rath tree.

...It is a humble, hidden house,
...The slender mane
of a yew-green tree
will show you where,
and the beauty around it
– great green oaks –
will make you certain.

Celtic monasteries in Ireland are eerily impressive, not only because of the beauty of their location, but by their isolation. Clonmacnoise in Co. Offaly looks over the great silver arm of the Shannon, while Glendalough in Co. Wicklow, beside its two lakes, is set among wooded hills. Legends emphasize the longing for solitude, away from worldly temptation, which was often personified in the form of a woman. Kathleen who pursued St. Kevin was thrown into Glendalough's upper lake for her pains. The small exquisite priory of Monaincha near Roscrea in Co. Tipperary, founded by St. Cainnech, was once an island located in the center of a great bog. Its aura had the power of killing any woman who made the mistake of attempting a visit.

I was fortunate enough to spend summers of my boyhood on a small island in the Kenmare river and learn that island life encompasses the outer world in miniature. The changing face of the sea, the lines of mountains in the distance, bird song, the scent of turf, downfalls of rain and fiery incandescent sunsets, all contributed to an enhanced feeling for landscape and nature. Tradition survived longer on islands. The Aran and Blasket Islands were the inspiration for a remarkable surge of literature and reminiscence early this century.

Over a thousand years ago asceticism was a moving force in Christianity and it was natural that saints and hermits should nurture it by seeking out the solitude of island life. Scores of little islands scattered in galaxies off the west coast still maintain some ecclesiastical evidence, a little roofless church or a hermitage, or the ancient cross on Tory Island off Donegal's stormy north coast.

St. Kieran built his church on the beautiful north face of Cape Clear, one of Carbery's Hundred Isles in Roaring Water Bay off Co. Cork, while the monks on the Skelligs sought the seclusion of the great cone rising out of the trackless sea. Remote Inishkea North and South, off Belmullet in Co. Mayo, are other minute islands chosen by anchorites who have left their traces in corbelled huts and cross slabs. Tory Island, site of some of the most lurid of Celtic myths, evolved into another location of hermetic Christianity.

Glendalough, County Wicklow

Clonmacnoise, County Offaly

The Stags, Broadhaven, County Mayo

The Skelligs, County Kerry

Inishkea South Island, County Mayo

Dún Aengus, County Kerry

Baltimore beacon and Sherkin Island, West Cork

Scattery Island, County Limerick

It has been said that the round tower is Ireland's sole contribution to architecture. Its purpose mystified nineteenth-century scholars, who even suggested that these towers had some sort of phallic association. Others thought that they were built by the druids or the Danes, or even the Egyptians. Since the Irish word for a round tower was *cloigtheach*, or bell-house, it is assumed today that they were free-standing belfries. At Clonmacnoise, Glendalough, Donaghmore in Co. Meath, Cashel and elsewhere, round towers stand by that other uniquely Irish stone monument, the high cross.

Earlier high crosses, like those at Killree, Co. Kilkenny, whose shafts and arms were joined by a ring, were decorated with elaborate designs recalling the Book of Kells. By the ninth century the decorations were turning increasingly to illustrations of episodes from the Bible. One of the most appealing of high crosses, with its combination of pattern and instruction, is at Moone in Co. Kildare. The Crucifixion is depicted, alongside twelve solemn-faced apostles and Daniel with his seven lions, all of whom jostle with other naïve figures, and stylized decoration that includes animals and dolphins.

Kells High Cross

High Crosses at Clonmacnoise, County Offaly

Monasterboice High Cross, County Louth

Moone High Cross

Jerpoint Abbey, County Kilkenny

Fore Abbey, County Westmeath

With the arrival of the Normans into Ireland, Christianity became more formalized. Often the new abbeys overlaid the old foundations. The ruins at Fore in Co. Westmeath constitute the best preserved Benedictine remains in Ireland, built beside the early monastery founded by St. Fechin, who died in A.D. 665. The Cistercian abbeys, Duiske and Jerpoint in Co. Kilkenny, Mellifont and Bective in Co. Meath, with their massive Gothic arches and cloisters, articulated the new age and a foreign element in Irish Christianity. Perhaps it was fitting that the headless trunk of the Norman conqueror of Meath, Hugh de Lacy, should be buried at Bective.

Sculpture turned from Bible stories on high crosses to effigies of knights and ladies in horned head-dresses. Among the cloisters of Jerpoint, Co. Kilkenny, a lady stands near her stone child. Not far away at Kilfane stands Ireland's most remarkable effigy, Cantwell, the long man of Kilfane. Eight feet in height, he holds a diamond-shaped shield decorated with rings and ermine tails that proclaim his family name.

> *Limestone strongman,*
> *Stone swaddled warrior,*
> *Knight ascendant,*
> *Kilkenny colossus,*
> *Alien Goliath,*
> *Slender magnificence,*
> *Cantwell fada!*
> *Awake O long man,*
> *Turn your head, Cantwell!*

Bective Abbey, County Meath

Murrisk, County Mayo

Kylemore Abbey, Connemara

Ferrycarrig, County Wexford

*C*antwell was a member of the Norman élite. It is said that the first Norman castle was constructed at Ferrycarrig in Co. Wexford to guard the mouth of the river Slaney. But Trim, begun a century later in Co. Meath, is the apogee of the golden age of castle building in Ireland.

> *Then Hugh de Lacy*
> *Fortified a house at Trim*
> *And threw a fosse around it*
> *And then enclosed it with a herisson*
> *Within the house he then placed*
> *Brave knights of great worth.*

A castle not only acted as a symbol of oppression, but in a physical sense was a marker delineating a territory. Castleroche in Co. Louth, with its great stone wall, held a strategic position between Ulster and Leinster, commanding an important pass leading into south Armagh. The most massive castles, at Dublin, Trim and Kilkenny, were strategic and defensive, designed as centers of power. Such fortresses were less likely to be associated with renowned Celtic hospitality. The older and more welcoming Dunguaire, overlooking Galway Bay, was described as

> *The white sheeted fort of soft stones*
> *Habitation of poets and bishops*

where, according to the Book of Lecon, King Guaire entertained all comers.

St. Canice's Cathedral, Kilkenny

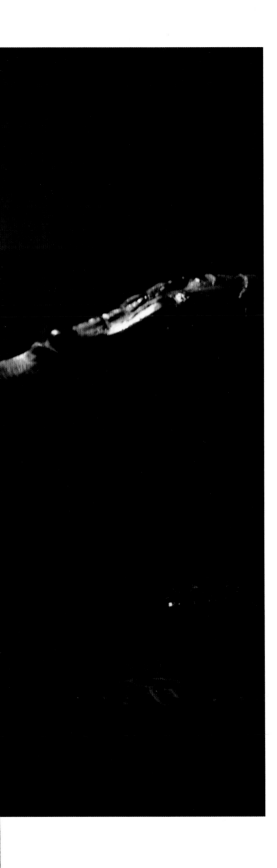

Mount St. Joseph, Roscrea, County Tipperary

Castleroche, County Louth

Doolin, County Clare

103

Trim, County Meath

Rathmore, County Meath

The Long Cantwell, County Kilkenny

The foreign takeover of Ireland initiated by the Normans confronted the rich cultural heritage that had evolved from Celtic belief into an idiosyncratic form of Christianity. Later conquests threatened the eclipse of Gaelic language and poetry and the destruction of tradition. That so much survived not only the overlay of Anglo-Saxon prejudice, but even the persecution of the nineteenth-century Roman Catholic Church, which had little sympathy for practises that had pagan roots, showed the tenacity of the old religion. But the Church knew how to compromise and Christianity continued to tolerate, if not respect customs that preceded St. Patrick.

In modern times these old traditions have been further weakened. But the respect for holy wells, pilgrimages, the penitential circuit of Lough Derg, the ascent of Croagh Patrick, are surviving aspects of ritual and belief reaching back for thousands of years.

Many simple rituals survive only in the form of superstition. Hawthorn, blooming in May, is unlucky to bring indoors. It is associated with fairies who meet at the thorns or live under them. If you put your clothes to dry on a lone thorn, you may be placing them over a fairy's washing. The decorated May bush has become a rarity, while the custom of putting green branches on the front door on May Day is also dying out.

The death of the wren was a Celtic ritual associated with the solstice. Today the children seldom make their circle on St. Stephen's Day as they once did, carrying a little dead bird.

The wren, the wren, the king of all birds
On Stephen's Day was caught in the furze.

Water bubbling from the ground is a natural source of mystery, and holy wells continue to be venerated. They can be found in every part of Ireland, small wayside shrines with nearby thorn bushes tied with pieces of colored cloth, attended by scatterings of coins, medals, rosaries, miniature statues and bottles of holy water. Our Lady's holy wells are hung with blue votive offerings.

Clerical suspicion of miraculous cures and the efficacy of water from holy wells was widespread. Protestant clergy in particular looked on in disapproval at such ceremonies as the pilgrimage to a holy well near Malin Head in Co. Donegal. Bishop Pococke, who saw the well in 1752, noted "the Roman Catholics plunge in with superstitious notions that the water carried some virtue from the Saint (Muirdhealac) who lived in a cave in the rock of a cliff". The frenzied climax of this pattern, when naked pilgrims plunged into the sea, washing off each other's sins, was a ritual that died in the nineteenth century. But a few other rituals with ancient pagan links are performed to this day. In north Cork, the well of St. Gobnait is a place of pilgrimage; Gobnait's holy day, like Brigid's, is in February, at a time of burgeoning fertility, and her pattern includes a ceremony which the priest avoids. Pilgrims still line up to measure the length of a blue ribbon against a battered medieval statue of Gobnait; the ribbon is then imbued with healing powers.

Many holy wells are dedicated to St. Brigid, and patterns were held in her honor which involved dancing and singing. The waters in her wells have healing powers which cure many ailments, from rheumatism to rheumy eyes, toothache and backache. At Liscannor in Co. Clare, her well and grotto display crutches discarded after cure.

May bush, County Carlow

Fishermen still keep a bottle of holy water in their boats as protection against the powers of the sea. At Kilmore Quay in Co. Wexford, after every funeral mourners place wooden crosses at a given station. Reverence of the pookas, spirits of rivers, lakes and mountains, is less; in my childhood, turf-cutters on the Wicklow bogs were still in fear of the spirit they called the Great Boo. Such animistic belief was more persistent in Ireland than elsewhere in Europe, and Christianity unwittingly preserved it.

Wren boys, Drumree, County Meath

St. Brigid's, Dundalk

Boat and bottle of holy water

St. Brigid's Holy Well, Mullingar

Kilmore Quay, County Wexford

Pooka

The World of Myth and Legend

Myth, legend and history often intertwine. Legends can be far more recent than the stories of the old gods. Near Glenade Lake in Co. Donegal the form of a giant otter is engraved on a stone, the Dab Hir or otter stone in Conwel grave-yard. The stone is said to recall an incident that took place in September 1772 when the death occurred of Grace McLoughlin, who was washing her clothes beside the lake. A monster climbed out of the water, killed her and began to devour her.

This was the fearful *dobharchú*, or otter, which local people feared as the monster of the lake. Her husband rushed to her aid and killed the beast, but its dying screams brought its mate to the attack. The husband's brother, Gilmartin, joined him in attacking the second otter, but they were forced to flee on horseback and barricade themselves in an outhouse, leaving their horses outside. The infuri-ated *dobharchú* mauled the wretched beasts until Gilmartin speared the monster in the neck and

Dobharchú, Lake Glenade, County Leitrim

killed it. So the husband and his brother claimed, and Grace McLoughlin's strange tombstone testifies to their story of the behavior of monster man-eating otters.

Lakes are sometimes melancholy places. On Lough Derravaragh in Co. Westmeath, the four children of Lir, bewitched by their wicked stepmother, were condemned to live out one spell of their exile as enchanted swans. "Children of Lir…from now on flocks of waterfowl will be your only family, and your crying will be mingled with the cries of birds." Of their nine hundred years as swans, three hundred were passed on Lough Derravaragh, where people flocked to hear their enchanted singing. When their enchantment was over, they were old, at the point of death; the only consolation in their sad story was the fact that they lived long enough to embrace the new religion of Christianity, recently arrived in Ireland.

Lake Derravaragh, County Westmeath

The Children of Lir

*L*ir was a member of the Tuatha De Danaan. His wife Eve bore him four beautiful children, Fionnuala, Aodh, and twin boys Conn and Fiachra. They loved their children dearly. Sadly, Eve died soon after the birth of the twins. So that the children would have a mother, Lir and his father-in-law King Bodbh Dearg agreed that Lir should marry his wife's sister, Aoife. The family were happy together for some time, but Aoife grew jealous of all the attention that the children received. She decided to get rid of them.

She set off in a chariot with the four children to King Bodbh's castle. On the way they passed a thick forest. Aoife ordered her servants to take the children into the woods and slay them. The warriors were shocked and refused to obey her. They warned Aoife of Lir's and the king's wrath. Aoife did not have the heart to kill the children herself.

They drove on to Lough Derravaragh, or the Lake of Oaks. It was surrounded by tall oak trees. Aoife invited the children to stop for a swim. When they were in the water, she drew out a druid's wand and chanted a spell. She cried out, "Children of Lir, your good fortune has ended. Henceforth you will live with flocks of birds and your cries will mingle with theirs."

The children were turned into four beautiful white swans. Terrified, they begged their stepmother to have mercy. She paid no heed to their cries. Fionnuala finally beseeched her, "O Aoife, if you will not restore us to our shape, at least put a time limit on the enchantment."

Aoife took pity on the children that she once had loved dearly. She answered, "I cannot break the spell, but know that you will not be swans for ever. You will stay on Lough Derravaragh for three hundred years, then you will go to the Sea of Moyle for three hundred years, and you will spend the final three hundred years by the Atlantic Ocean. You will become human again when you hear a bell chiming for a new faith. You will keep your own voices and minds and noble hearts. Your singing will be like music so sweet it will comfort everyone who listens."

When Lir heard that his children were missing, he rushed to King Bodbh. As he passed Lough Derravaragh the children were delighted to see his chariots and they called out to their father. At first Lir was puzzled, but he soon realized that the voices came from the beautiful swans on the lough. He was heartbroken when he saw what Aoife had done.

That night the children delighted Lir and his men with their music. Lir's great rage was calmed. The next day he continued on to King Bodbh's castle. There too waited Aoife. When the king heard of her treachery, he struck his daughter with the druid's wand. "For what you have done to the children of Lir I will turn you into a demon of the air." A sudden blast of wind swept Aoife up into the sky. Her shrieks and wailing may be heard still on a stormy night.

King Bodbh traveled back to the lake with Lir. Many nobles and people gathered from all over Ireland to hear the swans' lovely singing, and to tell stories. The music brought peace to anyone who was troubled. Over time, a community grew by the lake.

After three hundred years, Fionnuala told her brothers that they had to leave Lough Derravaragh to travel to the Sea of Moyle. The swan-children were very sad to leave all their friends and family. There was no one to hear their singing on the wild and remote sea-stretch between Scotland and Ireland. Once, a violent storm separated the swans, but they gathered again on Carraignarone, or the Rock of Seals. They were caught in ice, buffeted in gales and endured much suffering.

After many years, the swans flew to the Atlantic coast of Ireland. They flew over Lir's castle, but there was no fire to be seen nor trace of any building. Everybody at home was long dead. With heavy hearts they completed their last three hundred years of exile. Birds flocked from all along the west coast to hear their beautiful singing.

One day, from their island home of Inish Glora, the children were awakened by a strange sound. It was the ringing of a bell. It was rung by a holy man, a follower of Patrick, who had built a little church on a nearby island. The bell called him to pray each morning and evening. The swans realized their exile was over. They flew to the church and were welcomed by the Christian. From their singing he guessed that they must be the children of Lir, whose story had become legendary. "Your ordeal is over," he said. "A new religion of love has come to Ireland. Through it you will be freed."

Suddenly, he witnessed a most astonishing sight. Their feathers fell away and the swans were transformed back into human form. Tragically, nine hundred years had passed and now the children were old and wizened. The monk sprinkled holy water over their frail and feeble bodies. He gave them God's blessing and baptized them. They died peacefully soon after.

Rock of Cashel, County Tipperary

Carden's Folly, The Devil's Bit, County Tipperary

Not only the great figures of Celtic mythology make their presence felt in the landscape; the devil too is often an intruder. There have been many sightings of his satanic majesty. All over Ireland you will find devil's seats, bowls, feet, elbows and other parts of his anatomy as part of geology. High above Templemore in Co. Tipperary is the Devil's Bit, where the mountain has been gnashed by the devil in a fit of pique; he threw the morsel down onto the Tipperary plain where it stands as the Rock of Cashel. (But Cashel is limestone, whereas the rocks around the Devil's Bit are sandstone!)

A further devilish association is the little tower directly below, known as Carden's Folly. John Rutter Carden was a colorful nineteenth-century personality, who was jailed in Clonmel for trying to abduct a Miss Eleanor Arbuthnot after divine service. In addition, he was an evicting landlord known as the Tipperary Exterminator; to deter assassins coming to shoot him as he lay in bed, he had the staircase in his house removed. One of his good points, which he shared with the devil, was a liking for a good view. From the tower which he constructed under the Devil's Bit stretches a vast panorama of the Golden Vale, extending across to the Knockmealdown and Galtee ranges.

Martello towers were built along the coast of Ireland to defend English rule against a feared attack from French forces. The attack never materialized; many of the towers still stand. James Joyce lived for a short time in the Martello Tower at Sandycove, Co. Dublin, and chose it as the setting for the opening scene in *Ulysses*.

As a schoolboy I used to cross the creaking wooden bridge to Bull Island on Dublin's north side at Clontarf. To the north was the hump of Howth Head guarding Dublin Bay, and in the other direction the outline of the city. James Joyce walked these shores as a young man.

"A veiled sunlight lit up the grey sheet of water where the river was embayed. In the distance along the course of the slow moving Liffey masts flecked the sky, and more distant still, the dim fabric of the city lay prone in a haze."

The Battle of Clontarf, when Brian Boru died at the moment of victory over the Vikings, took place in 1014. It marked the end of the Viking wars, dashing their hopes of establishing their domination over Ireland. In Irish tradition it is sometimes referred to as "Brian's Battle"; the loss of such a hero, reputedly slain in his tent while kneeling in prayer of thanksgiving, was considered a great tragedy. Any account of the decisive Battle of Clontarf is a medley of myth and fact.

The fiery pirate queen Gráinne Ní Mháille, Grace O'Malley, was another warrior whose exploits have taken on the patina of legend. During her campaigns, she arrived one day at Howth Castle, where she was not welcomed. She kidnapped the lord's son, enticing him onto her ship. The conditions for his return were that an extra table setting should always be laid for dinner at the castle and the gates should be left open.

Slasher O'Reilly and Gunner Magee, whose mastery of the Irish guns in support of General Humbert at the battle of Ballinamuck made him legendary, have become more recent heroic warrior figures. On the Mayo coast, the stormy strand of Kilcummin is where a small seasick French army landed in 1798 to fight for Wolfe Tone's United Irishmen.

Opening scene of *Ulysses*

Stately, plump Buck Mulligan came from the stairhead, bearing a bowl of lather on which a mirror and a razor lay crossed. A yellow dressing-gown, ungirdled, was sustained gently behind him by the mild morning air. He held the bowl aloft and intoned:

– Introibo ad altare Dei.

Halted, he peered down the dark winding stairs and called up coarsely:

– Come up, Kinch. Come up, you fearful jesuit.

Solemnly he came forward and mounted the round gunrest. He faced about and blessed gravely thrice the tower, the surrounding country and the awaking mountains.

* * *

Haines asked:

– *Do you pay rent for this tower?*

– *Twelve quid, Buck Mulligan said.*

– *To the secretary of state for war, Stephen added over his shoulder.*

They halted while Haines surveyed the tower and said at last:

– *Rather bleak in wintertime, I should say. Martello you call it?*

– *Billy Pitt had them built, Buck Mulligan said, when the French were on the sea. But ours is the* omphalos.

Martello Tower, County Clare

Clontarf, Dublin

Ireland's Eye, Dublin Bay

Clare Island, Clew Bay, County Mayo, home of Grace O'Malley

Clew Bay, County Mayo

Finnea, County Westmeath, site of the heroic exploits of Slasher O'Reilly

Kilcummin Strand, County Mayo, site of the 1798 landing by the French army in support of the United Irishmen

There is something magical about the potato and the way that it can feed and sustain whole societies. Since it first emerged from the slopes of the Andes into the rest of the world, it has been associated with growth in population. This was the case in the west of Ireland, where it grew in particular abundance. High-potash manure was obtainable from seaweed along the coast, while the lazy-bed ridges which had been used for grain growing since Neolithic times were by chance ideal for the potato's cultivation.

When the potato failed there was a widespread feeling that malevolence was at work. At worst it was interpreted by those whom it suited as a punishment from God, a method directed from Heaven for reducing the population. The sprinkling of holy water among the blackening crops by terrified farmers is one of the most poignant images of the tragedy.

Doo Lough was the destination of a group of starving people who walked from Louisburg to Delphi; many perished in a storm that blew up as it does regularly. It is still a grim and lonely place, near the line of the Sheeffry Hills where the lake and changeable western weather combine in an atmosphere dominated by remoteness, physical beauty and austerity.

In the years after the famine an Englishwoman, Mrs. Houston, and her husband took a portion of land and farmed here. Mrs. Houston wrote of her life in a book called *Twenty Years in the Wild West*, an account dominated by a sense of loneliness and unhappiness. She herself was never threatened by starvation, but she witnessed much misery. The weather was the worst. "In nine seasons out of ten the sheaves of oat and barley stand as melancholy monuments of useless industry on the rain-soaked bogland till the grain grows in the ear and the crop is useless except for forage."

*S*outh of Kilcummin, a cross on the road to Delphi, overlooking the black waters of Doo Lough in Mayo, recalls a tragedy of the famine in 1846. Recent research has emphasized that the famine was less the result of the machinations of Cromwell and the behavior of wicked landlords, and more the fault of economic disaster. The crash of farming prices in the wake of the Napoleonic wars, and bad harvests combined with the failure of the herring shoals, brought the population to a perilous state. Then came the failure of the potato.

Sheeffry Hills, County Mayo

Ancient road, County Cork

Military road, County Wicklow

Bog road, Connemara

Blacksod Bay, County Mayo

Connemara

Connemara

Remote North Atlantic islands

Thousands of years before the famine, the hardships brought by the vagaries of weather moulded Celtic belief. It is unsurprising that myth and magic in Ireland should be so dominated by climate and landscape, or that the dominant gods and goddesses should be fierce, cruel and shrill like the weather itself. In physical terms lakes, islands, hills and mountains are filled with reminders of their deeds. In historical terms it has been suggested that some details of their make-up derive from Homeric Greece. Their rediscovery by Gaelic scholars like Douglas Hyde and poets like W. B. Yeats had a profound influence on the rebirth of Irish nationalism at the end of the nineteenth century.

Not all the great characters of Celtic legend were as unspeakable as Balor of the Evil Eye. Remote Tory Island off the coast of Co. Donegal was headquarters of the destructive cyclopedean god of the Fomorians. When the heavy lids of the huge eye were lifted, people died. He fortified the

eastern headland of Tory where the summit of the Doon peninsula is called Dún Balor, or the fort of Balor. His tower of glass from where he could spy out passing ships with a view to seizing them, no longer exists, but near the village of Gortahork there is a large boulder with a red crystalline vein said to represent the blood of Faoladh, whose head Balor cut off in a rage. The village of Clogha-neely derives its name from Cloch Cheannfaoladh (Stone of Faoladh's Head).

According to the sagas, Balor died on the plains of Moytura, slain by his grandson Lugh. His Fomorian followers were stationed to raise the lethal eye, but when the giant eyelid was at last creaked open, Lugh managed to kill him with his magical sling. The force of the stone drove the eye back through Balor's head and it landed in the midst of the Fomorian lines, killing hundreds of his followers with its evil power.

Moytura battlefield, site of Balor's death

Balor of the Evil Eye

*B*alor was the most powerful king of the Fomorians, a terrible pirate people who were enemies of the learned Tuatha De Danaan. Balor lived on Tory Island (Island of the Tower) off the wild north coast of Ireland. The place where his glass tower stood is still called Dún Balor, or the fort of Balor.

One day when he was quite young, Balor passed a druid's house and heard chanting inside. Curious to see what was happening, he climbed up and peered in the high window. The room was filled with smoke and poisonous gases. There were several magicians standing in a circle.

Suddenly there was a small explosion in the center of the room and fumes billowed straight out into Balor's face. Blinded by the gases, his face stinging, Balor fell to the ground. He found he could not open one eye. A druid stood over him as he lay outside the house. "That smoke was made from a spell of death. Your eye now has the power to kill. Anyone you look at with that evil eye will die."

Balor's grandson

*W*hile he was king, Balor was told by a druid that his own grandson would kill him. To insure that this could never happen, he locked his only daughter, Eithlinn, in a tall stone tower on his island, with twelve women to guard her. They were never to mention a man's name. With these precautions, Balor felt safe.

Eithlinn grew into a beautiful woman. But she often felt lonely. Meanwhile, Balor continued to raid the Tuatha De Danaan. He stole a valuable cow from the noble Cian. Cian went to a witch named Biróg for help. She disguised Cian as a woman. The two arrived at Eithlinn's tower and the women guards let them in out of the storm. Biróg put a sleeping spell on the guards, while Cian ran to Eithlinn's room. At once Eithlinn realized that she had been lonely for such company. They immediately fell in love, but were brokenhearted when Biróg swept Cian away the next morning before Balor discovered them.

Eithlinn was very sad but delighted when she gave birth to her lover's son. She named the child Lugh. Balor was horrified. He determined to kill the baby straightaway. The child was taken from his mother and carried to the shore wrapped in a blanket held together by a pin. The women guards dropped the child into the sea. The pin opened and the baby rolled free into the waves. This bay on Tory Island is still known as Port Deilg, or Port of the Pin.

Balor believed that his grandson was drowned. The witch Biróg had been close by, however. She lifted the child out of the water and brought him to his father, Cian. As he grew, Lugh learned many skills. He would need these in the final combat with his grandfather. After slaying Balor by slinging a stone into his eye, the hero Lugh led the Tuatha De Danaan to fight and overcome the Fomorians.

Near Sligo on the bay is Ben Bulben, where Diarmuid was killed by an enchanted boar. In her retelling of Celtic legends, *Over Nine Waves*, Marie Heaney tells how "At the summit of the mountain he flung Diarmuid from his back and as the man lay on the ground he gave a mighty spring on to him, and gored Diarmuid with his tusks and ripped the entrails out of his body … Diarmuid made a last valiant cast with the hilt of the broken sword … the creature … fell on the hillock not far from where Diarmuid lay. To this day that place on the mountain top is called Rath na hAmhrann, the Rath of the Sword Hilt."

Ben Bulben is associated too with W. B. Yeats, many of whose poems celebrate the beautiful Sligo countryside. The Text of "The Stolen Child" is commemorated at Glencar Waterfall. The haunting chorus sounds

Come away, O human child!
To the waters and the wild
With a faery, hand in hand,
For the world's more full of weeping than
you can understand.

South of Sligo, Queen Maeve's presence is found on Knocknarea, topped by Maeve's Cairn. Maeve is an enchantress associated with the fairy world. In her human form she is considered a greedy and devious woman. Among the locations that echo her name and the wonders she performed is the Poisoned Glen in Co. Donegal, known as Maeve's Foul Place.

Rathcrogan in Co. Roscommon has numerous traces of the goddess-queen. Rings, mounds, barrows, a pillar stone and other half-hidden places scattered over a twenty-acre site include the cemetery of the kings, the Hillock of the Corpses and the location of Maeve's palace. There are also caves, one of which is an entrance to the Underworld. On All Saints' Day (1st November) spirits fly out of it like a swarm of bees. You can just squeeze yourself into Cruchan's Cave below the lintel scratched with Ogham writing and look out at the sky.

Perhaps Queen Maeve is best known as the fiery protagonist in the convoluted legend of the great bull of Cooley. The saga tells of Cuchulainn's stand against the power-hungry queen and the battle between the forces of Connacht and the Ulstermen centered at the great Navan fort, with its ringed enclosure and wooden palace, which had to be conquered by force of arms or magic. Outside the ramparts the men from the west crouched and beat at the ramparts with their feet and fists, flinging up dead leaves and thistles.

Not far from Navan in Co. Louth died the arrogant and ultimately tragic hero Cuchulainn, tied to the Clochafarmore standing stone. It is entirely fitting that the death of the greatest Irish hero should be linked with a standing stone, a humble archeological yardstick which follows on from the early course of Irish prehistory. Cuchulainn's death has been well-chronicled, from the time he received his mortal wound, and the moment when he used his belt to bind himself to the stone so that he would meet his death standing up, his feet on the ground. When a raven appeared on his shoulder, his enemies knew he was dead.

Ben Bulben, County Sligo

The Pursuit of Diarmuid and Gráinne

*T*he hero Finn Mac Cool, as an old man, *desired a wife. The young and beautiful Gráinne, daughter of the king of Ireland, Cormac Mac Art, was brought to him. Gráinne loved the handsome and charming Diarmuid O Duibhne, one of the Fianna, Finn's followers. During the banquet feast that evening, she gave Finn a sleeping*

potion to drink. Cormac and most others at the table also drank from the goblet.

While they were sleeping, Gráinne told Diarmuid she loved him. He replied that he would not defy Finn's wishes. But Gráinne placed a spell or strict obligation upon him to take her away from Finn and her father. Diarmuid protested that he was loyal to Finn, but Gráinne insisted. Finn's son Oisín and grandson Oscar were sorry for Diarmuid, but told him he had no choice but to go with Gráinne. To break the obligation would bring doom. Diarmuid's druid friend feared that Gráinne would be the cause of Diarmuid's death. Diarmuid wished his friends a sad farewell.

Finn awoke the next morning. He was enraged when he heard of the elopement. He set off in pursuit with his followers and dogs across Ireland. They soon traced the pair to a wood in Connacht. As the parties confronted each other, Aengus Og, Diarmuid's guardian from the ancient Tuatha De Danaan, suddenly appeared. He spirited Gráinne to Limerick while Diarmuid remained behind to escape honorably or die at the hands of his friends. After Diarmuid's escape, he followed Gráinne to Limerick. Aengus gave them advice to keep moving always.

Thus began the legendary pursuit as Diarmuid and Gráinne traveled all around the country. Many places in Ireland, caves and rocks, are named after the lovers seeking shelter. Several times they came very close to capture. Finn's followers managed to sound a warning so that they might move away or hide, but Diarmuid faced all dangers bravely.

Eventually, Aengus asked Finn and Cormac to make peace with Diarmuid. They agreed, with certain conditions. After sixteen years of pursuit, Diarmuid and Gráinne lived happily and prospered on an estate, known as Rath Gráinne, or Gráinne's fort, in Keshcorran. They had five children, four boys and a girl.

Gráinne decided to invite Finn and Cormac to a reconciliation feast. The festivities went on for a year. Towards the end of the feast, Diarmuid was woken by the sound of hunting. As the Fianna were not allowed to hunt on the estate, Diarmuid went out to investigate. He reached Ben Bulben mountain. There sat Finn. He told Diarmuid that hunters were chasing the wild boar of Ben Bulben and warned Diarmuid to escape as it had been foretold that Diarmuid and the boar would be the death of each other.

Diarmuid stood his ground and soon the wild boar came thundering up the mountain. Man and beast fought together. Finally, Diarmuid killed the boar at the place known as Rath na hAmhrann, or the Fort of the Sword Hilt. Mortally wounded, Diarmuid lay alongside the creature. Finn could not hide his pleasure. Oscar berated his grandfather. Diarmuid implored Finn, who had magic powers, to bring a drink to heal him. Reluctantly Finn went to the well nine feet away and cupped his hands to bring the water. As he returned slowly, he opened his hands a little and the water slipped to the ground.

A second time Finn tantalized Diarmuid. But the third time he was too late. Diarmuid was dead. Oscar knew that Finn had set this trap for Diarmuid. The Fianna followed Finn down Ben Bulben to Gráinne, while Diarmuid's close friends mourned their loss.

When Gráinne, who was heavily pregnant, heard the news, she fainted and fell out over the ramparts of their castle. Her triplets were born dead on the spot. There was terrible wailing and lamentation.

Three hundred Tuatha De Danaan carried away Diarmuid's body to the Otherworld.

After some time, Finn went to Gráinne and courted her with fine talk. Finally she agreed to be his wife. Her children joined the Fianna. The pursuit of Diarmuid and Gráinne was over.

Glencar, County Sligo

147

Queen Maeve's Mount, Knocknaree, County Sligo

Cruachu, County Roscommon

Owenynagat, Cruachu cave (entrance to the underworld), County Roscommon

Oisín and Tír na nÓg

One day when the Fianna were out hunting, a beautiful woman on a white horse came riding up. Finn asked her who she was. She replied that her name was Niamh. She was the daughter of the king of Tír na nÓg, the land of youth. Niamh confessed that she loved Oisín, Finn's son. She invited him to accompany her back to the land of youth. She described a wonderful kingdom, splendid with gold and marble and beautiful gardens. Oisín was entranced by Niamh's beauty and by her eloquence. He agreed to travel to Tír na nÓg. Finn bid his son a sad farewell.

Oisín and Niamh sped away on the tall white steed. They rode across seas and past cities and forests, far away. Oisín had never seen such places before. They encountered some dangers. After a very long journey, they arrived at the kingdom of Tír na nÓg.

The king and queen were delighted to see their daughter safe, and welcomed Oisín to their land and home. The country was truly wondrous to behold. There were beautiful trees and flowers. The people dressed in white and gold robes. Sweet music played, and there was singing and laughter everywhere. Stories were told, and poetry was recited. Oisín was amazed at such beauty and harmony.

Oisín and Niamh were married. The wedding feast lasted for ten days. They had three children, two boys and a girl. The family was very happy and content. No one grew old in that land.

After a time that seemed like three years, Oisín grew homesick. He asked Niamh and the king if he could visit his father and the Fianna in Ireland. Niamh went pale. "I fear you will never return," she cried. Oisín promised her he would be back soon. He would ride on the white horse who knew the way.

Niamh's final caution was that Oisín must not dismount from the horse or let his foot touch the ground. Otherwise he would not be able to return to Tír na nÓg. Weeping, she beseeched him not to go. "Everything is changed in Ireland. You will not find your father," she warned.

Oisín tried to reassure her. He rode away, and after a long journey he was back in Ireland. Three hundred years had passed in the time he was away. He met a crowd of people who stared at him curiously. He asked them of the whereabouts of Finn Mac Cool and the Fianna. They shook their heads and replied, "These are characters from long ago. They are legends."

Oisín was dismayed. He realized that centuries had passed. He rode to Almu, once the home of the Fianna. No castle remained, only a lonely and overgrown hill. With a heavy heart, Oisín sadly turned away.

At Glen na Smole, or the Valley of the Thrushes, he saw three hundred people attempting to raise a huge marble stone. Men were being crushed by the weight. They called to Oisín for help. With his hero's strength, Oisín raised the marble and flung it off the men. But with the strain, the horse's strap broke, and Oisín was thrown from the saddle. The moment his feet touched the ground, the horse bolted. The crowd gasped as the handsome and strong young warrior withered before their eyes into a helpless, blind old man flailing on the ground.

The men carried Oisín to the Christian missionary, Patrick. Patrick preached the new gospel to the old man, but the proud warrior scorned the bishop's message. Defiantly, Oisín celebrated the lives of Finn and the Fianna that he loved.

The Death of Cuchulainn

By the time he was twenty-seven, Cuchulainn had many enemies, among them Erc and Lugaid. The most dangerous were the six grotesque, shape-shifting children of the magician Calitin, whose father Cuchulainn had killed during the Cattle Raid of Cooley. Queen Maeve still resented Cuchulainn's success in that battle. She determined to avenge the deaths of her warriors.

The children of Calitin agreed to help her. They declared that within three days they could bring Cuchulainn to his doom. King Conor heard this ominous news and ordered Cuchulainn to come to his castle for his own protection.

The children of Calitin came to the castle and tore up the ground around it to resemble a battle site. They wished to provoke Cuchulainn to fight. His friends tried to restrain him, telling him that it was all a wicked illusion. After a second similar attempt to delude him, it was decided by his friends that Cuchulainn should go with the lovely Niamh to a remote valley out of harm's way. But the children of Calitin sought him out, spying his horse, the Gray of Macha. They tried again to persuade the warrior that he was under attack by a great army. When this failed, a daughter of the magician took on the shape of Niamh. She then exhorted Cuchulainn to go out to face the army of Connacht. In amazement at this change in character, he agreed.

As he prepared for war, many bad omens put a secret dread on the hero. Three old hags asked him to eat the flesh of a hound. This was forbidden to Cuchulainn because his name meant Hound of Culann. However, he ate the meat and his usual strength left his arm and leg.

Erc and Lugaid set up a series of false fights of honor between two warriors, with a druid pretending to decide the outcome in each case. The druid tricked Cuchulainn to hand over his spear or else he would dishonor his good name. It was foretold that this spear would kill a king. The first time Lugaid threw it at the great warrior, it hit and killed Cuchulainn's king of charioteers. After a second false combat, the druid was handed the spear, as Cuchulainn would not dishonor the good name of Ulster. Erc threw it back and the noble horse Gray of Macha was wounded. For a third time a false challenge was staged and Cuchulainn handed over the spear to avoid dishonor to his countrymen. Lugaid snatched it and flung it with all his might. It pierced Cuchulainn's armor.

As the warrior lay dying, he asked if he could get some water. They allowed him to crawl to the lake nearby. He did not have the strength to return to his enemies so he dragged himself erect and tied himself with his belt to a pillar stone on the shore of Baile's Strand. Cuchulainn would die on his feet facing his foe. Lugaid and the others cautiously approached. The Gray of Macha galloped up to his dying master and scattered his enemies. Dripping sweat and blood, the horse then went to Slieve Fuad to die.

For three days the enemies watched the hero. At last a raven settled on his shoulder and they knew he was dead. Lugaid cut off the warrior's head. The sword in Cuchulainn's hand slipped from his death grip and sliced off Lugaid's hand. The tragic hero's body was left tied to the pillar stone on the strand.

Cuchulainn's stone, County Louth

*T*om Kelly has managed to catch the moment of Cuchulainn's death with a cloud hovering over the Clochafarmore stone in the shape of a winged bird. Kelly's patience and passionate enthusiasm has meant that all the landscapes in this book are imbued with magic and myth. His pictures blend the artist's skill and the accumulated knowledge of a countryman, with his reverence for the ancient forces of nature. He captures the effects of drizzling rain, a sharp autumn wind stirring the leaves, or the changing forces of the sea. He traps the moment when a phosphorescent sunset begins to change, and chases the rainbow which is the sling of the sun god, Lugh. He touches on history and the ruins it has left as he seeks out castles, monasteries, round towers and ecclesiastical buildings, all of which have contributed to legendary Ireland. These pictures are a homage to artists in stone, past mysteries and the Celtic gods that lurk behind the island's Christian façade.

As Turner tied himself to the mast of a sailing ship in order to experience and then paint a storm, Kelly has spent many lonely vigils in the countryside waiting for the moment to record transitions of light and land and seascape. Above all he respects the forces of nature:

> *We are shattered and battered, engulfed*
> *O King of clear-starred Heaven!*
> *The wind has swallowed us like twigs*
> *Swallowed in a red flame out of Heaven...*